CLIMATE

Torrey Maloof

CW00411247

Published by Pearson Education Limited, 80 Strand, London, WC2R 0RL.

www.pearsonschools.co.uk

This edition is published by arrangement with Teacher Created Materials, Inc. for sale solely in the UK, Australia and New Zealand.

© 2015 Teacher Created Materials, Inc.

Text by Torrey Maloof

22 21 20 19 18
10 9 8 7 6 5 4 3 2 1

British Library Cataloguing in Publication Data
A catalogue record for this book is available from the British Library

ISBN 978 0 435 19464 2

Copyright notice
All rights reserved. No part of this publication may be reproduced in any form or by any means (including photocopying or storing it in any medium by electronic means and whether or not transiently or incidentally to some other use of this publication) without the written permission of the copyright owner, except in accordance with the provisions of the Copyright, Designs and Patents Act 1988 or under the terms of a licence issued by the Copyright Licensing Agency, Barnards Inn, 86 Fetter Lane, London EC4A 1EN (www.cla.co.uk). Applications for the copyright owner's written permission should be addressed to the publisher.

Printed in China by Golden Cup

Acknowledgements
We would like to thank the following schools for their invaluable help in the development and trialling of the Bug Club resources: Bishop Road Primary School, Bristol; Blackhorse Primary School, Bristol; Hollingwood Primary School, West Yorkshire; Kingswood Parks Primary, Hull; Langdale CE Primary School, Ambleside; Pickering Infant School, Pickering; The Royal School, Wolverhampton; St Thomas More's Catholic Primary School, Hampshire; West Park Primary School, Wolverhampton.

The author and publisher would like to thank the following individuals and organisations for permission to reproduce photographs and illustrations:
Photographs
(Key: b-bottom; c-centre; l-left; r-right; t-top; bck-background)
Cover Front: Getty Images: Shishic/iStock/Getty Images Plus/, Back: **123rf:**kenishirotie, **Shutterstock** :Suppakij1017 b.
Alamy Stock Photo: Juniors Bildarchiv/R304/Juniors Bildarchiv GmbH 11, Imagebroker 14, Dennis Cox 15, Peter Bisse/Stock Connection Blue 20, **Getty Images:** Pixac/iStock/Getty Images Plus 4-5bck, Imagedepotpro/E+ 8- 9bck, Robynmac/iStock/Getty Images Plus 10-11bck, Raisbeckfoto/iStock/Getty Images Plus 13, LucynaKoch/ iStock/Getty Images Plus 14-15bck, RyersonClark/iStock/Getty Images Plus 22-23bck, Mlenny/E+ 24-25bck, Flip Nicklin/Minden Pictures 25, Anna Henly/DigitalVision 27,BenGoode/iStock/Getty Images Plus 26-27bck,Yekorzh/ iStock/Getty Images Plus 30, AlexSava/iStock/Getty Images 31, **NOAA:**19, **Science Source:** Gary Hincks 7, **Shutterstock:** NH 3bck, Torwaistudio 5, Natalia Bratslavsky 6-7bck, Deer boy 9, Galyna Andrushko 12-13bck, Sergioboccardo 16, Chantal de Bruijne 16-17bck, Alex Tihonovs 18-19bck, Creative Travel Projects 20-21bck, Fekete Tibor 21, Alex Polo 22, HitToon 28, BlueOrange Studio 32.
All illustrations: Teacher Created Materials(TCM).

Note from the publisher
Pearson has robust editorial processes, including answer and fact checks, to ensure the accuracy of the content in this publication, and every effort is made to ensure this publication is free of errors. We are, however, only human, and occasionally errors do occur. Pearson is not liable for any misunderstandings that arise as a result of errors in this publication, but it is our priority to ensure that the content is accurate. If you spot an error, please do contact us at resourcescorrections@pearson.com so we can make sure it is corrected.

Contents

Weather and Climate

What clothes will you wear tomorrow? It will probably depend on what the weather is like. If it is warm and sunny, you might wear shorts and a T-shirt. If it is cold and windy, you might bundle up in a scarf and coat. Weather changes from day to day and from place to place.

What if you wanted to plan what to wear next term? You would need to know about the climate. Climate is the weather pattern generally found in a place.

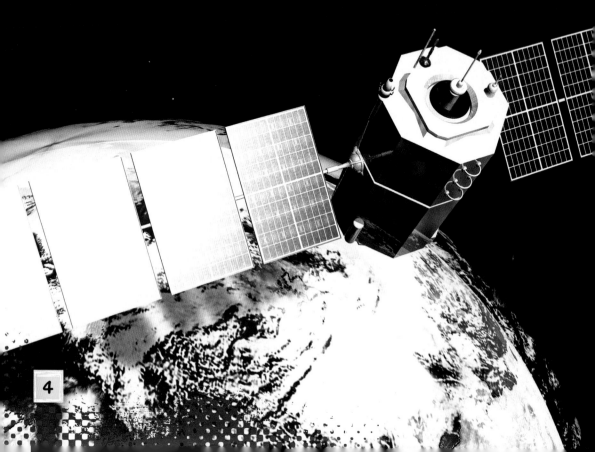

If we want to know what the climate will be like in the future, we need to understand what causes changes in the climate.

Using Computers

Scientists use information about past weather to predict how climates will behave.

Lots of different things can affect the climate. For example, the amount of **moisture** in the wind can make a difference. If there's only a small amount of wind, without much moisture, the climate will be dry.

Mountains affect climate too. They force the air to rise. Because of this, we can end up with a wet climate on one side of a mountain, but a dry climate on the other side.

Oceans affect the climate as well. They add moisture to the air. Oceans can also store heat from the sun. This affects the **temperature** of the air near oceans.

Scientists have to think about all of these things when they are describing an area's climate. They also look closely at the plants and animals that live in an area. These can tell scientists a lot about climate.

Rain Shadow

A rain shadow is a patch of land that has become dry because mountains block rainy weather. As air rises up the side of a mountain, moisture is squeezed out. When the air falls on the other side, it is dry.

Climate Zones

Earth is divided into different climate zones, or areas. There are three main types of climates. They are low-latitude climates, mid-latitude climates and high-latitude climates.

- Low-latitude climates are closest to the **equator**. They are usually very warm.

- Mid-latitude climates are further away from the **equator**. They are not too cold or too hot. These are **mild** climates.

- High-latitude climates are the furthest from the equator. This group includes the North and South Poles and other very cold places.

Let's look at these climate zones more closely.

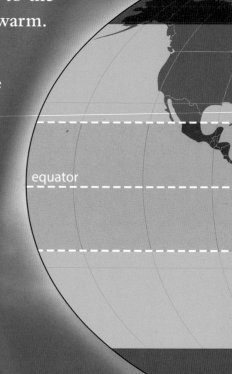

equator

The **equator** is an imaginary line that runs around the middle of Earth.

Purple areas show high-latitude climates.

Green areas show mid-latitude climates.

equator

Orange areas show low-latitude climates.

Low-latitude Climates

Areas near the equator have warm, sunny climates. Many people love to go to these places on holiday.

Tropical rainforests

Tropical rainforests are near the equator. As well as being sunny and warm all year round, it is also humid. When it is humid it means there is a lot of moisture in the air. It rains a lot in the rainforest.

This warm, wet climate is the perfect **environment** for plants to grow. There are many different types of plants in the rainforests, such as ferns, mosses and huge trees.

The highest branches on these trees form a **canopy**. The canopy acts like a roof for the rainforest. Millions of insects and animals live under this roof.

There are more types of living things in the climate of a rainforest than any other place on Earth. Colourful birds fly through the trees. Snakes slither around the forest floor. Monkeys swing from branches, and frogs leap from place to place. You may even see other animals, such as jaguars or kinkajous.

ferns

a kinkajou

moss

Rainforests only cover a tiny amount of Earth, but about half of Earth's plants and animals live there!

Savannahs

Savannahs are large, flat areas of land, covered with grass and a few trees. Parts of Africa are savannahs, and if you visit them you might see elephants and zebras roaming freely. You might spot a giraffe drinking water from a pond, or even a family of lions!

Nearly all of the animals that live in the savannah eat grass.

Savannahs are found between rainforests and deserts. The weather is warm all year round.

In this climate, there is a wet summer season. It rains a lot for a few months. Then there is a long dry winter season. During the winter, there is not much rain, but there are lots of lightning storms.

Our original home

The first humans lived in the African savannah.

an acacia tree in Tanzania

Deserts

Most desert climates are hot. In fact, the ground gets so hot that it heats the air. You can actually see the air rise in waves. These waves can play tricks on your eyes. They make people see things that are not really there. This is called a mirage.

Many deserts are sandy and very few plants grow there. This is because deserts are dry. During the winter months, deserts get very little rain. Sometimes, it's so hot that the rain evaporates. This means that the rain turns from water into a vapour, or gas, before it ever reaches the ground. This leaves hardly any water for plants and animals.

Although it is very hot during the day, at night it gets very cold in the desert. Plants, animals and people in the desert have to live with very high and very low temperatures.

Animals like the rock hyrax can live in the desert.

Watching the winds

When dust is blown for millions of years, it leaves behind ridges in the land, like these in China.

These ridges are used for farming in China.

Mid-latitude Climates

Areas further away from the equator are milder. These are popular places for plants and animals – including humans – to live.

African governments have created national parks to preserve the beautiful grasslands.

Which is which?

Grasslands are very similar to savannahs. So how can you tell the difference? Grasslands tend to have fewer trees – and more grass!

Grasslands

Grasslands are large, flat areas of land that are covered in different types of grasses. These areas do not receive enough rain for tall plants, such as trees, to grow. Without trees to break the wind, grasslands can be very windy places. If the soil becomes too dry, it can blow away. Over time, this can turn a grassland into a desert.

Most of the soil found in grasslands is good for farming. Crops such as wheat and corn grow in grasslands.

Many animals love to eat the grass. Bison and antelope can be seen in grasslands. Farmers will often keep sheep and cattle on grassy land.

Grasslands in the UK

There are different kinds of grasslands in many parts of the UK. In our grasslands you might see butterflies and crickets, as well as birds such as woodlarks, lapwings and nightjars.

Mediterranean climates

Mediterranean climates are found close to the sea. This climate has four seasons. Winters are cool and moist. There is not much rain, and even less snow and ice. Summers are warm and dry.

Plants in this climate have **adapted** to help them survive. For example, in the dry season, there are fires. Some plants have seeds that stay hidden in the ground until there is a fire. The seeds crack open in the heat from the fire, and new plants grow from the seeds.

Parts of Australia, Chile, the west coast of the USA and South Africa have Mediterranean-like climates.

Amalfi Coast, Italy

Sea changes

Scientists can find out about the climate by studying changes in the sea. They use small robots called Argo floats to collect **data**.

Mild climates

Mild climates have four different seasons. To tell which season it is, simply look at the leaves on **deciduous** trees. There are small green leaf buds in spring, and larger green leaves in summer. The summers are not very hot and it rains on and off throughout the year.

In autumn, leaves change to beautiful shades of orange, red and brown. In winter, the leaves fall off the trees. This cycle helps trees stay alive during cold winter months.

Animals have to survive cold winter months too. Some animals in the UK, such as hedgehogs, dormice and bats, do this by hibernating. This means they spend the winter hiding away and sleeping. Other animals, like birds, migrate. This means they move to warmer climates for the winter.

This North American black bear can hibernate in its warm den for up to seven months without food.

Revealing rings

Every year, a tree grows a new ring in its trunk. The rings may be thinner or thicker depending on temperature, rainfall and other factors. These rings show important changes in the climate.

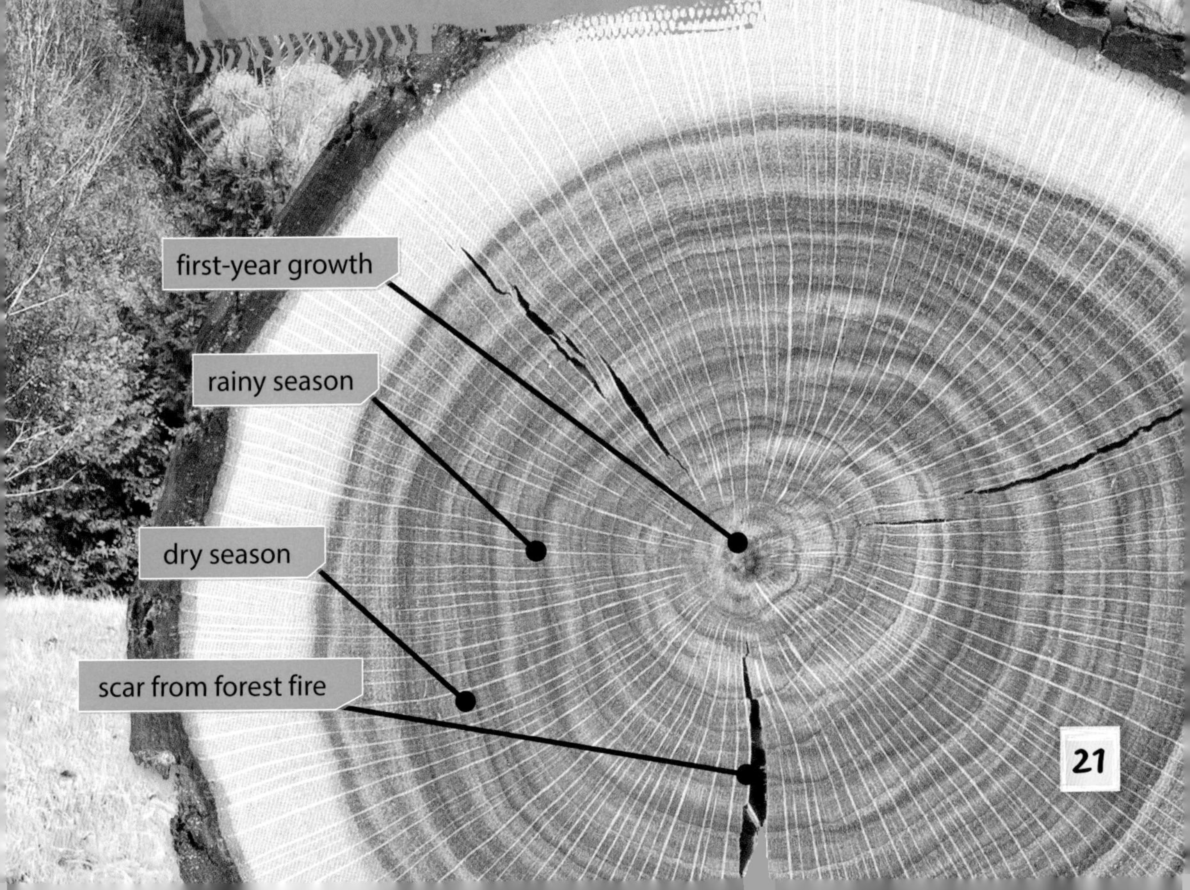

first-year growth

rainy season

dry season

scar from forest fire

High-latitude Climates

The climate in high-latitude areas such as the Arctic and Antarctic is very cold. These areas are very much affected by climate change. This means big differences in the normal weather conditions of a place over a long time.

A muskeg is a boggy place that can form in sub-arctic areas.

Sub-arctic climates

Sub-arctic climates have short, cool summers and long, very cold winters. Some areas with this climate are humid, while others have very little rain. There is a lot of snow. In fact, a layer beneath the soil or rock is frozen all the time. It is called permafrost because it is permanently frozen.

The taiga forests that grow in this cold climate are very thick. The trees include spruce, pine and fir. The dark green colour of the trees helps them absorb sunlight. These trees have needle-shaped leaves, filled with a watery juice called sap. This helps keep the trees from freezing during long, cold winters.

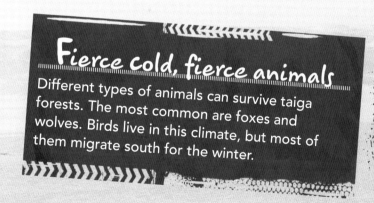

Fierce cold, fierce animals

Different types of animals can survive taiga forests. The most common are foxes and wolves. Birds live in this climate, but most of them migrate south for the winter.

The arctic tundra

If you think taiga forests in the sub-arctic are cold, try living in the arctic tundra! This is the area of the Arctic Circle that surrounds the North Pole. The climate is extremely cold there.

Winters are long and dark. For several months, there is no sunlight. There is a very short mild season, but no real summer. During this time the sun is out for 24 hours a day!

There are no trees in this area because of the extreme cold, but there is some plant life.

You may think that there are no animals in this cold environment, but you would be wrong! There are caribou and arctic hares, foxes and wolves. There are even animals that live in chilly waters, such as walruses, beluga whales, seals and polar bears.

beluga whales

Climate Change

Today, scientists are observing many changes in Earth's climate. They have noticed that it is getting warmer. The overall temperature on Earth is rising faster than normal. Most scientists think human behaviour has caused this and other extreme changes. Grasslands are turning into deserts, and tundras are melting. Many places have more powerful storms and longer dry periods. This adds water to the oceans and causes the water level to rise.

Scientists around the world are collecting more data. They want to study the causes of climate change so they can slow it down. Together, they are finding ways to protect climates that are home to plants, animals and humans all over the world.

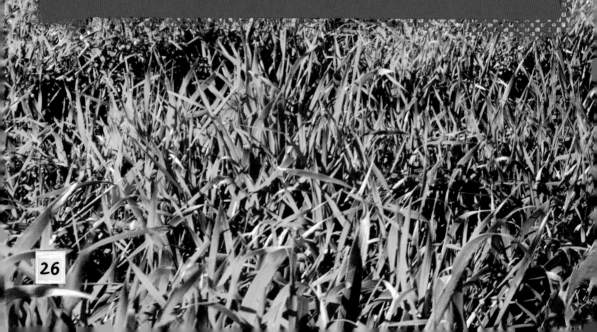

This glacier in Greenland is melting because of the unusually warm weather.

Let's Try It!

How do clouds form? Try an experiment and find out!

What you need

- food colouring
- hot water
- ice cubes
- large, clear jar
- small plate
- stopwatch

What to do

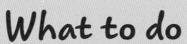

1 Ask an adult to heat some water and pour it into the jar.

2 Add a drop of food colouring to the water.

3 Cover the jar with the plate. Let the jar sit for a minute. Look in the jar. What do you see?

4 Place ice cubes on the plate. Observe for a minute or two. What do you see?

Glossary

adapted – changed so that it is easier to live in a particular place

canopy – the highest layer of branches in a forest

data – information

deciduous – trees that lose their leaves every year

environment – an area where something exists or lives

equator – an imaginary line around the middle of Earth

latitude – distance north or south of the equator

mild – not harsh

moisture – tiny droplets of water in the air or on a surface

temperature – a measure of how hot or how cold something is

Index

Your Turn!

Create a Climate

What climate do you live in? How do you know?
If you could create your ideal climate, what would it
be? What would the weather be like? What plants and
animals would live there? Draw a picture of your climate.